AWAKENING

A DREAM JOURNAL

AWAKENING

A DREAM JOURNAL

ELLEN FOREMAN, Ph.D.

A JANE LAHR ENTERPRISE

STEWART, TABORI & CHANG
NEW YORK

Design: Jeff Batzli
         J.C. Suarès
Consulting Photo Research: Natalie Goldstein

88 89 90 91 92 9 8 7 6 5 4 3 2 1

Library of Congress Cataloging-in-Publication Data

Foreman, Ellen.
    Awakening : a dream journal.

    "A Jane Lahr Enterprise."
    1. Dreams.   I. Title.
BF1091.F67   1988   154.6′3   87-26753
ISBN 1-55670-031-8

Published in 1988 by Stewart, Tabori & Chang, Inc.,
740 Broadway, New York, NY 10003
Distributed by Workman Publishing,
708 Broadway, New York, NY 10003

Printed in Japan.

COVER: *Aspiration*, commissioned in 1928, detail.
Augustus Vincent Tack.
FRONTISPIECE: *Above the Mountain Peaks*, 1917,
Paul Klee.

DEDICATION

A dream not understood is like a letter not opened.
The Talmud

To Rhys Caparn, my teacher.
J.L.

To my Monday dream group—Claire, Diana, Elaine, and Pamela—who explore with me the profound mysteries of the dream world.
E.F.

Evening Star III,
1917, Georgia O'Keeffe.

ACKNOWLEDGMENTS

I would like to express enormous gratitude to the Knoedler Gallery—especially Lawrence Rubin, Cam Newel, and Carol Corey—whose effort and assistance made this book possible.

I would also like to thank the following friends for their help in creating this book: Natalie Goldstein, John Lynch, Jane Bassin, Ruth Marten, Cristina Salat, and Mr. S. Crites, who proved to me for all time that dreams can come true.
J.L.

I am deeply grateful to Maureen Graney, my editor, whose sympathetic understanding and constructive suggestions have strengthened this book immeasurably.
E.F.

CONTENTS

NOTES ON THE PICTURE SELECTION

A *dream* is a little hidden door in the innermost and most secret recesses of the soul, opening into that cosmic night which was psyche long before there was any ego-consciousness. . . . It is from these all-uniting depths that the dream arises, be it never so childish, grotesque, and immoral. So flowerlike is it in its candor and veracity that it makes us blush for the deceitfulness of our lives.—**Carl Jung, "The Meaning of Psychology for Modern Man"**

SINCE THE BEGINNING OF TIME, EVERY HUMAN BEING HAS SLEPT, dreamed, and awakened to wonder at the strange, rich visual worlds encountered in dreams. We have all experienced surprise at our own inner landscapes after a night of particularly vivid images.

In preparing this book, we felt a dynamic visual component was essential. It is our wish to honor the visions that flow from the unconscious in form of *symbol* as well as *dream* and to pay tribute to the power of these images. The artists among us have brought forth numinous, compelling, and astonishing works from their dreaming minds to their waking lives. Their messages can lead us to new perceptions of ourselves and the world we live in.

The works of art were selected to facilitate an inner dialogue. If there is one outstanding visual theme in our choices it is the mandala, a symbol that occurs in all cultures. Jung tells us that the object of a mandala is "the self in contradistinction to the ego, which is only the point of reference for the consciousness, whereas the self comprises the totality of the psyche altogether, *i.e.*, conscious and unconscious" (*Mandala Symbolism*). So the mandala is a visual form representing the integrated state, and we believe it

Ex-Libris Page of Shah Jahan, 1628–1658, Indian.

Stela of 'Ofenmut:
detail of *'Ofenmut
Offering before Horus,
Sun's Barque above*,
ca. 1991–1786 B.C.,
Egyptian.

can be an active guide toward that state. The artwork in this book
has a meditative, unitive quality. Being open to the power of the
images may well bring you toward the point of integrated
awareness, the mandala being an agent in that transformation. One
of the most stunning examples of the active capacity of the mandala
is found in the exquisite sun rosette detail from the seventeenth-
century Indian illuminated manuscript leaf.

Throughout these introductory pages are artistic symbols from
ancient cultures—Hindu, Egyptian, Native American, and Islamic.
These cultures have traditionally believed that the divine manifests
through dream and symbol, an insight that modern man has lost. In
reclaiming our lost sense of soul and our profound urge toward
wholeness we can turn to these ancient images for inspiration. The
rest of *Awakening* celebrates the visions of twentieth-century artists such as O'Keeffe, Dove, Tack, Motherwell, and Diebenkorn,
artists with a deep-rooted respect for symbol whose works demon-
strate an ongoing dialogue with their psyches. These painters were
often inspired by the art of ancient cultures and have drawn
authority from the same creative well. We have not included
paintings of dreamers dreaming or dream images. Instead we have
chosen works that will set the tone for a journey toward personal
integration, which is the underlying aim of this dream journal.

An ancient Gnostic gospel teaches: "If you bring forth what is
within you, what you bring forth will save you. If you do not bring
forth what is within you, what you do not bring forth will destroy
you" (Gospel of Thomas, 45.30–33). From deep within, dreams act
as signposts, directing our attention toward what we need to bring
forth. Let these images act as catalysts for a process that can
become an astonishing journey toward transformation.

Jane Lahr

INTRODUCTION

Once upon a time,
I, Chuang Tze, dreamt I was a butterfly, fluttering hither and thither, to all intents and purposes a butterfly. I was conscious only of following my fancies as a butterfly and was unconscious of my individuality as a man.

Suddenly I awakened and there I lay, myself again.

Now I do not know whether I was then a man dreaming I was a butterfly, or whether I am now a butterfly dreaming I am a man.—**Chuang Tze**

OUR FASCINATION WITH THE WORLDS OF SLEEP AND WAKING ENDURES. Which experience is more real? Which is "illusion," which is "reality"? When are we most awake? What is the relationship between our sleeping and waking selves? How can our dreams be used in our waking lives?

Since ancient times, philosophers and poets, kings and slaves have grappled with the questions of what dreams are and what they mean. Indeed, in ancient societies dreams were thought to be the work of gods and spirits, presenting dreamers with messages from another realm. Used to prophesy, to cure illness, to reach new insights, to solve problems, dreams have traditionally been honored and taken seriously.

With the Western world's growing emphasis on scientific inquiry and its validation by empirical phenomena, the dream was devalued. Today we still say, "Oh, it was only a dream." At the turn of the twentieth century, developments in the new field of psychoanalysis, led by Sigmund Freud, brought the dream back to respectability. Freud was the first to attempt a comprehensive explanation of dreams and the way they could be interpreted. He believed that

Eye Panel, detail of *Coffin of Khnum-nakhte*, ca. 1991–1786 B.C., Egyptian.

dreams were the keys to the innermost secrets of the personality, that each presented a "royal road to the unconscious." He recognized the unconscious as the motivating source for all behavior and thought, thus uncovering the significant relationship between dreaming and waking life.

In the last thirty years, exciting breakthroughs have been made in our understanding of that relationship. Scientists seeking to understand the nature of sleep have offered us intriguing information about the process of dreaming. In sleep labs, volunteers have been hooked up to electroencephalograph (EEG) machines so that the patterns of the sleeping mind could be meticulously charted. We have learned that sleep is far from a passive state. Sleepers move through four distinct stages of sleep, starting with stage one, a light sleep in which brain waves most closely resemble those of the waking state, and ranging to the deep sleep of stage four before we begin to drift back up to stage one again. This pattern recurs throughout the night in ninety-minute cycles.

The most fascinating part of this research is that the return to stage one is marked by rapid eye movement (REM): the eyes move quickly beneath the closed eyelids as if they were watching an event. Subjects awakened from REM sleep almost always report that they have been dreaming. These REM periods lengthen throughout the night, taking up more of the ninety-minute cycle and producing longer dreams. Researchers have found that although dream imagery occurs during non-REM sleep as well, the most vivid, compelling, and easily remembered dreams occur during REM periods.

Dream imagery is not limited to sleep; it also occurs in those twilight stages between waking and sleeping, sleeping and waking. The worlds of waking and sleeping drift into each other, each affecting the other. The mood we are in as we go to sleep affects our dreams, and our dreams of the night affect our daytime mood.

But for all the physiological data, the dream remains elusive. What is a dream? Why do we dream? Do dreams have meaning? There are many theories but no definitive answers. Perhaps mystery is essential to this process because it challenges us to grapple with our dream images as we struggle to find meaning in our total life experience.

Ceremonial Robe, nineteenth or twentieth century, Native American (Chilkat, Tlingit).

Spurred on by the scientific breakthroughs and by exciting discoveries about the right side—the creative side—of the brain, interest in learning to use dreams to improve waking life has increased. "Dream work" is being used to help people solve problems, achieve goals, make decisions, and gain greater insight into themselves and the world they live in.

Some dream workers approach the tasks alone, others with a partner, still others in a group. Contemporary dream work takes many forms. All over the world dream groups have sprung up, allowing people to share their dreams in order to appreciate and understand them.

This book presents a new, personal, and very flexible way of thinking about and approaching dreams. The guiding idea of the text is that the dream not only reflects the dreamer but can be a powerful tool for change. The personal symbol glossary at the back of the book encourages you to track the development of dream images recurring over time. The accompanying workbook is a specially designed journal that will function like a responsive dream partner. Both glossary and workbook are invaluable components of dream work, reflecting like a mirror the transformations going on in your internal world.

Writing itself is a powerful creative tool. Converting the dream experience from a vague collection of fleeting images to concrete language is the first step in the creative process of dream work. The workbook, or dream journal, becomes a way of focusing yourself, and in rereading you will learn to listen to yourself.

I recommend keeping a dream journal for at least several years so that you can see the emerging patterns and watch your own growth. As you become more aware of the real concerns of your life and your ways of dealing with problems, you will find yourself in a dynamic dialogue with yourself that will bring your inner and outer worlds into mutual partnership.

In this book, we approach dreams on their own terms. The idea is to allow dreams to speak in their own language—through their own images, structure, and logic—and to treat them like other products of imagination—like works of art, poems, and plays. Dreams are intricate works of beauty, elegance, and complexity, not codes to be reduced to a simplistic message. Dreams have meaning on many levels simultaneously, and the longer you work on a dream, the more it has to offer you. The multiple meanings are "teased out"

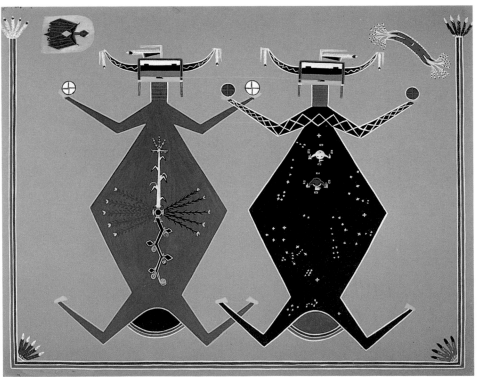

and expanded as you play with them. As you develop your skills, you will learn to appreciate the individual creativity of your own dreams. There are myriad ways in which the inventiveness of your dreaming mind spins out, night after night, elaborate stories and multiple characters, powerful metaphors and witty puns, in its attempts to make sense of your world and experience. Dream work is an art. There are no hard and fast rules. Like an artist, you will have to learn to trust your intuitions because only you can discover the true meaning of your dreams. The exercises in this book will help you improve your recall and will suggest ways to record your dreams. They also suggest ways in which your waking interests and intentions can send messages to your dreams so that you can get specific help and guidance. Dreams are spontaneous expressions offering a deeper level of awareness and insight than our daytime selves allow. We can learn to work *with* our dreaming mind, but if we try to control and manipulate it, we forfeit its wisdom.

This book is arranged sequentially so that you can experiment with different approaches and ways of thinking about dreams as you accumulate written dreams to work with. In the final chapter, I encourage you to go beyond the dream, to create different endings to your dreams, to find alternate solutions to problems, and to express the dream artistically. You will find that some dreams lend themselves to one approach rather than another. Being flexible is crucial.

Whether you are an experienced dream journalist or are writing down your dreams for the first time, I know that awakening to your inner self will put you in touch with your own often surprising creativity. Your waking self will be enriched to the degree that you explore your dreams. Your journey begins on the first page of your journal.

TOP: *Hiranyagarbha*, ca. 1775–1800, Kangra School, Indian.

BOTTOM: *Shooting Chant*, No. P-4 #4A, undated, Native American.

CHAPTER ONE

CATCHING YOUR DREAMS

If I were sitting here describing a dream . . . there'd be a certain look on your face. And I know what that look means because I feel it myself— recognition. The pleasure of recognition, a bit of rescue work, so to speak, rescuing the formless into form. Another bit of chaos rescued and "named." It's as if you just saved someone from drowning. And I know the feeling. It's joy.—**Doris Lessing, *The Golden Notebook***

IT CAN BE EXASPERATING. ONE MOMENT YOU ARE CAUGHT UP IN A DRAMATIC situation of such immediacy and intensity that the experience feels more real than most events in everyday life. You awaken and the same images, so alive and compelling a moment before, are already fading like ghostly apparitions, leaving only traces of feeling. We must catch those fleeting images.

We dream involuntarily, but retrieving those dreams requires an act of will. Some of us even assert that we never dream. The fact is that everyone has four or five dreams every night—but not everyone is lucky enough to remember them without practice. Some techniques can help you overcome the obstacles by improving your recall so you can record your dreams and begin a creative dialogue with the dreaming part of yourself. Dreams respond best if your waking self is receptive, and the more welcoming your attitude is, the more the dreaming mind will respond.

Dreams have provided inspiration for artists, musicians, poets, scientists, and inventors. The creative potential of our own dreams is available to all of us, but tapping it requires a positive attitude and strong desire. Remind yourself as you are going to sleep that you *do* dream and that tonight you will remember your dreams and write them down.

Circular Forms, detail, 1930, Robert Delaunay.

Do not underestimate the power of suggestions made just before sleep. Your unconscious will pick them up to process, and your dreams will respond to the attention. It may take some time, anywhere from a few days to a couple of weeks, before this process achieves results, but patience and persistence will be rewarded. Keep your journal and a pen or pencil within easy reach, at the same place by your bedside, every night. At bedtime, open the journal to the next blank page and place next morning's date at the top.

The dream you are most likely to remember will be the last dream of the night, which usually occurs just before you normally wake up. Sometimes a dream may awaken you during the night.

When you awaken from a dream, lie still and play it back, letting its images make their impression on your mind. Grasp all images, even if they seem trivial. Fragments are important in themselves and can often encourage more information to come to the surface.

If you have a "feeling" of a dream without its images or story, try shifting your body, simulating various sleep positions. Dreams seem to surface in the position in which they were dreamed, as if the body contained the memory. To trigger the memories, try thinking about significant people in your life, or of yesterday's events, or of current problems you are facing. Write your dreams down as soon as you have replayed them. Train yourself to write in the dark if you wake up spontaneously during the night. Practice makes this easier. Use a penlight or let the finger of your opposite hand serve as a guide as you write by marking off approximate line spaces along the side of the page. In the morning you may well find a record of dreams you have no recollection of writing down. If you find writing during the night too intrusive, try dictating your dreams into a tape recorder and later transcribing them into your journal.

To preserve their immediacy, record your dreams in the present tense ("I am walking down Broadway . . . .") with as much detail as you can recall. Record everything—conversations, emotions, thoughts, images, people, colors, locations—no matter how weird or incongruous they seem at the time. Try to record the events in chronological order, to preserve the structure of the dream. Sometimes a color in the dream, or whether the dream is in color, is important and should be noted. If there are powerful images that are hard to describe, use the margins of your journal to draw them.

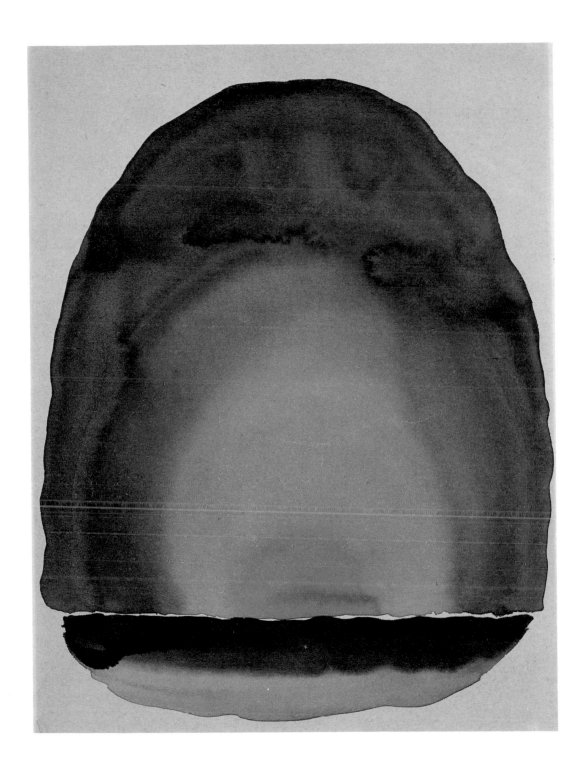

In writing the dream, let the words spill out spontaneously. Let the flow of the dream carry you on. Sometimes you will find yourself having difficulty finding the right word. This is important. Give yourself time to find the word that fits most precisely. One dreamer recorded, "I found myself lost on city blocks." She used "blocks" instead of "streets" and that choice felt very important to her. In interpreting her dream she realized it was the key: the dream was about feeling blocked.

Use a word even if it feels strange to you. Don't correct it. It may be very significant. Where one dreamer might ordinarily have described his situation as "living on a hill," he found himself writing "living on a bluff." Indeed, he discovered that he felt he was being fraudulent in his professional life. Our dreams often use puns that can provide us with the key to their meaning.

Though it is best to write down a full dream during the night, simply noting some of the dream's images will give you enough material to work with. If you record a dream in the morning, or when you write out your dreams more completely, ask yourself:

〰 What were my feelings about the dream upon awakening?
〰 What are my immediate associations to the dream?
〰 What events of the day before might have triggered the dream?
〰 What events am I anticipating the next day that may be reflected in the dream?

Record your responses in the journal to set the context for each dream. If you wake up naturally, rather than being jarred awake by the buzz of an alarm, you increase your chances of dream retrieval. For many people the weekend is the best time to record dreams because waking is leisurely and immediate concerns of the day do not quickly crowd out the night's images.

When you capture as much of a dream as you can, celebrate your success by giving your written dream an appropriate title. This is the next step in working with the dream. Single out some aspect that seems outstanding—an unusual character, place, or situation, a unique image, a new phrase—that best names the dream. To name this dream, the dreamer chose the image that she felt was most striking.

Mary is laying out Tarot cards, twelve in a row. Each card represents an operation she will perform simultaneously. She is a surgeon. I am amazed at the sense of skill she shows. I notice one card is a shy, dark, young Ethiopian woman with a distended belly. I think she is pregnant. Mary is to operate, to cut her open. I wonder aloud to Mary if the Ethiopian child-woman even realizes that she is pregnant.

To this dreamer, the title "The Pregnant Ethiopian" seemed appropriate. The ambiguous image of a possibly pregnant woman whose belly is distended like that of a starving child revealed the dreamer's fear that she might be incapable of "feeding" her own original conception, which was a highly ambitious project. She had undertaken to write a book and saw this project as her "baby," as writers often do. She both wished to be and feared being delivered of this project prematurely.

Titling gives each dream its own identity and individuality, and helps you find its cohesive themes. Even more important, a good title helps you recall the entire dream when working on your personal symbol glossary and when discovering series of dreams.

Oriental Garden, 1925,
Paul Klee.

There is no "proper" title to a dream. The choice is uniquely your own, and it is important that *you* title your dream.

Another important aspect of naming dreams is that it allows them to move closer to plays, poems, movies, and stories, their natural heirs, and makes them more accessible to you as creative works. Think of your dreams as first drafts of a creative work, and they may then serve as inspiration.

- Develop a positive attitude toward your dreams.
- On going to sleep, remind yourself to remember your dreams.
- Keep your journal at your bedside every night.
- Make note of any images recalled; even fragments are important.
- Recall and write your dreams as they flow, in words and phrases; do not worry about correct grammar.
- Let the dream speak to you in its own language.
- Make associations between your dreams and the context of your daily life.
- Give your dream a title.

TAKE IT PERSONALLY
Creating Your Own Personal Symbol Glossary

N*o dream symbol can be separated from the individual who dreams it, and there is no definite or straightforward interpretation of any dream.*—**Carl Jung**, *Man and His Symbols*

WHERE DO DREAM IMAGES COME FROM? AT OTHER TIMES, AND IN OTHER cultures, it was believed that dreams were messages from the supernatural—from the gods, the Devil, ancestors, or spirit guides. Modern theorists suggest that the dream is a communication from one part of the self to another part, the unconscious to the conscious, the dreaming mind to the waking mind. If so, these messages are a most sophisticated form of personal communication.

Most of our dream images come from our everyday experience, but are arranged and combined in new, sometimes fantastic ways by the unconscious dreaming mind to give fresh insight into a situation or problem. Our culture provides a vast common store of images from which we can draw, yet the images we *choose* to represent our dream thoughts and the particular ways we use those images are charged with unique personal significance. No dictionary but your own can define what the stories and images in your dreams mean to you. Other dream dictionaries can only suggest ways in which images have been interpreted in other people's dreams (and in fact may suggest new associations your dreams may later use). Each dreamer employs a unique vocabulary, grammar, syntax, and logic. By creating your own symbol glossary, you can become aware of the personal significance of events, images, and combinations of images in your dreams. Particularly significant symbols tend to appear repeatedly, almost demanding your attention.

No. 1, White and Red, 1962, Mark Rothko.

Cosmic Sun, 1915, Theo
van Doesburg.

Any object, person, or animal in a dream can have powerful emotional associations. It may simultaneously represent an aspect of yourself. One woman dreamed of "a piece of luggage, scruffy, showing signs of wear, frayed but still usable and serviceable." Upon examining her associations, she realized with shock that she was describing hidden feelings about her life: the piece of luggage was a symbol for herself. She felt knocked around by life, but still intact and useful.

Dream images try to call your attention to issues below your level of awareness. In doing so, each image has many, even contradictory, meanings. When an image is strong or puzzling, try to think of what it *may* mean, what it suggests, instead of what it *does* mean. Draw on the context of the dream and on associations with your waking life to reach the feelings evoked by each image.

One dreamer, Barry, found many powerful images in a dream he called "The Red Sweater." His sometimes puzzling associations with the images provided the keys to a very apt interpretation.

I'm in a house or apartment. My ex-girlfriend Ruth is in her bedroom taking an afternoon nap. I go into the room and want to make love to her. I sense she is involved with another man. She's wearing a red, oversized pullover sweater.

From this dream, Barry chose six images that he felt were most provocative. He sensed that they were related to one another and to his current life situation. He free associated:

House or apartment: permanent or transient? past or present?
Her bedroom: separate from me; private; alluring.
An afternoon nap: vulnerable yet inaccessible; luxurious and forbidden; passive, not taking responsibility.
Sense she is involved: all in my head; cut-off response; defended.
Red sweater: toreador's cape, inviting but deadly dangerous; scarlet woman = adulteress; red will draw you like fire.
Oversized pullover: the other man's sweater; his claims on her.

Landscape (The Hare),
1927, Joan Miró.

In working on the associations to discover the dream's meanings, Barry uncovered a deep ambivalence: he was still powerfully attracted to an old, painful experience. He questioned why he should have this dream now, more than a year after the relationship had ended. Anniversaries are a powerful mobilizing force for dreams, and he remembered that her birthday was coming up. In the dream he felt he should not have been there in the room, but he had not yet walked out and closed the door. He realized that the feelings were more than he was able to handle at the time of the breakup and that he was still in the process of resolving his emotions. The dream made him aware of how tentative he was in approaching new relationships for fear of being betrayed again.

He entered in his personal symbol glossary the images and meanings that had most resonance for his life. He wrote in, for example, "Red sweater, 3/21/88: sexual seductiveness associated with Ruth." In later dreams Barry used a similar process, selecting, free associating, deriving meanings from both the contexts of the dream and his current life. He added images and their meanings to his glossary and paid particular attention to any recurrent images. He dated each entry, and watched for change and development. A meaning that seemed fixed at the time of a dream may no longer seem so weeks or months later.

There are no hard and fast rules for choosing images. Images may feel provocative, significant, disturbing, puzzling, mysterious.

Choose those that resonate within you. Everything in a dream has the potential to carry meaning, but for practical purposes, do not get carried away. If you miss a highly significant image, it will probably reappear. Remember:

Golden Storm, 1925, Arthur G. Dove.

- ⤳ Explore images that feel most provocative to you.
- ⤳ Sense the image's meanings through its relationship to other parts of the dream.
- ⤳ Free associate to your chosen image.
- ⤳ Ask yourself why you had that dream *today*.
- ⤳ Record recurring images and their associations with dates in the alphabetized glossary.

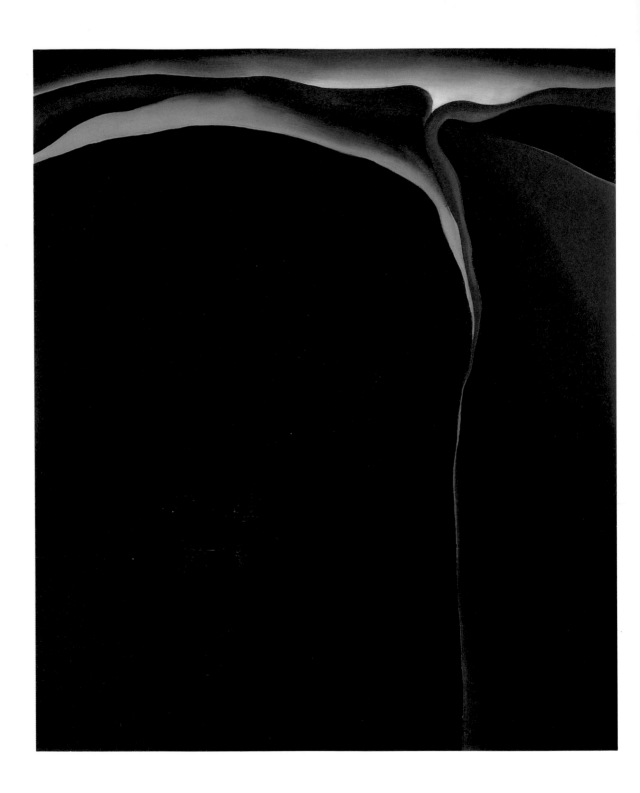

CONFRONTING THE CONFLICT

O*n the night before [Caligula's] assassination he dreamed that he was standing beside Jupiter's heavenly throne, when the God kicked him with the great toe of his right foot and sent him tumbling down to earth.*—Suetonius, *The Twelve Caesars*

AT THE CENTER OF EVERY DREAM LIES A CONFLICT HIDDEN FROM WAKING life, an unresolved problem. Most of the dreams that we remember spontaneously are highly charged emotionally and occur at times that are most stressful. Dream research shows that the more conflicts we are experiencing in our daytime life, the more dream sleep we need. The dreams are attempts to resolve the conflicts. They offer new perspectives, which we may not be aware of in waking life. The conflict expresses itself as a theme in the dream. Look for tension or conflicting elements that may be symbolized by characters, situations, or opposing feelings. Conflict is embedded in the dramatic structure of the dream.

People often ask what they can do about nightmares, which are, ironically, our most often and most clearly remembered dreams. Sleep researchers have distinguished between night terrors and nightmares. Night terrors occur during non-REM sleep and usually are remembered as one frightful scene, such as being attacked. They leave too little imagery to be worked with constructively. Nightmares are nocturnal anxiety attacks and, like other REM dreams, contain complex imagery. They leave such an intense imprint that they are remembered both on being awakened and in the morning. Nightmares can be treated in the same ways as other dreams in identifying and resolving conflicts and problems.

Dark Abstraction, 1924, Georgia O'Keeffe.

PAGES 36-37: *Thunder Shower*, 1939–1940, Arthur G. Dove.

The source of the dream's conflict may be difficult to determine, but it is important to remember that it always does reflect conflict in our waking lives. If you can connect the conflict in a dream's theme with a real-life conflict, you have a key to the dream's meaning and, more important, keys to understanding and resolving a major issue in your life.

Take, for example, the dream a young psychologist had the night before her meeting with a dream group. She ended up presenting this very dream, which she called "The I Test," to the group.

I walked into the hospital where I worked. A nurse told me to call the doctor in the eye department. I called him. He had a kind, calm, warm voice. He said, "We need to retest your vision. You have a special odd type of contact lens." (It had an inner eye in the lens: an inner circle and an outer circle. I feel embarrassed.) The tests had been for people with ordinary lenses. I did the retest.

I'm looking through pictures of myself. On each is stamped DEVOID. Among the pictures were the results of the retest, also stamped DEVOID. I realized I hadn't passed, not quite 20/20. I'll have to get my contacts readjusted.

In examining the context of the dream, the psychologist recalled that she had spoken on the phone the night before the dream to the doctor—a colleague—who leads the group, and she immediately felt that the dream anticipated her imminent presentation in front of the dream group.

Once the contextual connection is made, the dream—rich in symbols, puns, and other possibilities—begins to unfold. It reveals the dreamer's conception of the dream group as a hospital, a place to seek treatment. But there is a conflict of roles: she is a colleague of the group leader, a professional who works in the same field, so why does she become a patient just by presenting a dream? She is concerned with her identity (the eye equals the "I," or self, department), and her dream presents the image of a "very special odd contact lens." She fears and hopes that she will be judged differently from the other members of the group who do not work in the field of psychology (the "ordinary" members). She wonders if she is in the inner circle, and wonders, too, about her inner self and whether she will be found wanting.

Red Light, Spherical Composition, ca. 1923, Ivan Kliun.

With the contextual connection made, the dream opened a range of possibilities. The dreamer was able to see in a new way her unconscious attitude toward her personal and professional identity, her contact or lack of contact with others (she needs her "contacts" readjusted), and the competitive world in which she lives, judges herself, and is judged by others. This powerful new perspective can now be used in her waking life.

The "I Test" dream also shows that a conflict of immediate concern, her worry about the next day's presentation, may also reflect larger issues in the dreamer's life and personality. A current situation can act like a trigger, setting off memories of similar situations or events and calling upon the dreamer's characteristic strategies for dealing with such issues.

We all have complicated lives, with multiple conflicts going on simultaneously, and of course the tricky question is how to find the right context in our lives. Which of the areas is relevant? The dream itself provides the clue. In "The Red Sweater" Barry knew the conflict referred to his emotional life because the dream was about his ex-girlfriend, who no longer was present in his daily life.

Song, 1958, Kenneth Noland.

Another clue was the timing: the ex-girlfriend's birthday was approaching. In trying to establish the contextual connection, it helps to recall what you were thinking about just before you fell asleep.

To confront the conflict presented in your own dreams, ask yourself:

↝ Do the contextual notes I made when I recorded my dream provide a clue?

↝ What are my immediate associations to the dream?

↝ What events and thoughts of the previous day may have precipitated the dream?

↝ What immediate events am I *anticipating* that may be relevant?

Once the connection between nighttime image and daytime event is made, the dream yields new perspectives. You can now explore how the specific situation and your response may reveal your characteristic behavior pattern. Maybe this exploration will help you notice how this pattern operates in other areas of your life so you may begin to resolve areas of conflict.

LOGICAL ILLOGIC
The Logic of Dreams

D*AUGHTER:*
. . . it's all a dream I've dreamed. POET: It's all in a poem I once wrote. DAUGHTER: Then you know what poetry is. POET: I know what dreams are. What is poetry? DAUGHTER: Not reality. Something more than reality. Not dreams, but wide-awake dreams.—**August Strindberg,** *A Dream Play*

DREAMS SEEM FORMLESS, CHAOTIC, AND RANDOM BECAUSE THEY DEFY commonsense, linear reality. But every dream is an effort by the dreaming mind to reveal something new about the dreamer's everyday experience. A dream is like an internal memo written in a private shorthand.

The language of the dream is not the language of literal, logical, practical discourse, but the language of poetry. Dreams flout the laws of Aristotelian logic, which state that *A* is *A* and not *B*; an automobile is an automobile and not a boat. In a dream you can be driving a boat-car that later turns out to be an airplane.

The dream has its own laws. Its logic is poetic, encompassing novelty, contradictions, and ambiguity; far more is permissible than in everyday life. Think of your dream as a film in which there are startling scene shifts, flashbacks, characters appearing both the way they are and the way they were.

How does this logical illogic work? Everything in the dream—characters, setting, props, dialogue—is meaningful, and everything is symbolic. And looking specifically at those elements that seem illogical or that do not quite fit can show you the key to the dream. Perhaps the illogical elements have associations with things that *do* fit; their metaphoric identity can open up new angles of vision. A metaphor allows *A* to be somehow the same as *B* and at

Dancing Elegy, 1984, Robert Motherwell.

the same time to be something new; it pulls together formerly disparate elements to form a new entity, a new concept. For example, if you dream of man *A* but call him man *B*, you may be observing, for the first time, an aspect of man *A* (such as hostility) that is symbolized by man *B*.

The compression of two images into one can reveal the similarities underlying the disparity of our experience and can elucidate and magnify connections we were only dimly aware of in waking life. Metaphor gives a dream amazing range, allowing it leaps of freedom, the crossing of boundaries, the transcendence of conscious and unconscious observations to show their interrelationship. We are shown the familiar in the unfamiliar, and the unfamiliar in the familiar. Like putting a new lens on a camera, examining our dreams opens up startling new perspectives. An artist frustrated by yet another rejection of a grant proposal had a dream she called "My Mother, Myself." Examining the apparently illogical compression of two people into one provided her with the key to the dream's meaning.

I'm having a conversation with my mother in which she expresses my frustration with being an artist and with the point of view of not being recognized by the people around me. I feel grateful and relieved. The scene is an interior where I grew up. I am a younger, longer-haired me. My mother is a kinder mother than the one I had, and looks like an older me. It is like me talking to me.

The mother in this dream is not like the artist's mother at all, and the artist is not her real adult self. The artist realized that she feels young, as if she is just starting out and has a lot of growing up to do, yet she also feels she can offer herself the mothering solace she so needs. Metaphorically, she is her own mother.

A common illogicality in dreams is envisioning yourself as you are today, but finding yourself in a childhood setting. This could suggest that you are feeling like a child in a certain situation. It might also suggest that your present conflict has its roots in childhood. Approach these illogicalities with a kind of experimental openness, trying out different possibilities to see what fits.

Metaphorical associations are crucial. Even when the images seem to be mundane, they are in fact saturated with the personal feelings and attitudes they represent. Even a TV set or a pair of

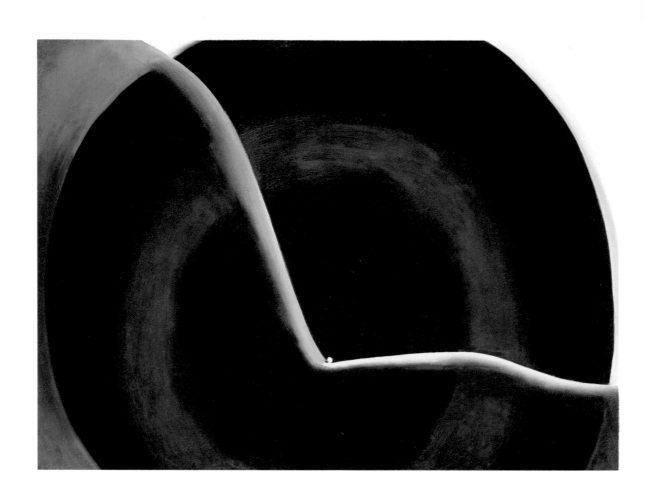

shoes can illuminate the emotional tone of a dream. More often, though, strange images or names appear, seemingly out of nowhere.

The occasion of a dream called "Jacome" was the dreamer's birthday, which she spent with her husband, Arthur, and four friends who function in her life like an extended family. The three couples had spent the summer together traveling in a bus. The day had not been very special because her "family" of friends had not seemed to know what she wanted or needed and had been preoccupied with their own concerns. The dreamer juxtaposes her own disappointing "family" experience with the ideal extended family of the girl who gets what she is looking for.

I am in a souvenir-type gift shop, looking for some "jacome." I can't find it on the shelves, but a young Hispanic woman I am with finds a lot of stuff she wants. Paying takes a lot longer than we anticipate since she has to pay a value-added tax. We must rush back through the desert. It becomes dark and dusty and she leads the way. Arthur and the others are waiting with impatient expressions on their faces. People are hanging out in front of the bus waiting for us. As soon as they see us, they scamper on the bus.

The dream was a mystery until the dreamer associated the made-up word "jacome" with the surname, Jacoma, of a Hispanic student she knows whose extended family works together to help one another. The dreamer felt that her friends had let her down (or "deserted" her) on her birthday, and she realized that she wished for the kind of family support the student had. The dream expressed her disappointment and her unfulfilled wishes. You can best unravel the logic of your dreams by paying attention to those very areas that seem most illogical.

↝ Look for metaphors and try to see the area of similarity that you have not noticed before.
↝ Ask what a dream character means to you in your waking life and what aspect of yourself you identify with that character.
↝ Be open and play with the possibilities.

The most seemingly illogical aspects will take on perfect logic.

SEEKING THE SERIES

A *single dream* reflects one vista of the mind. A series of dreams reveals the whole panorama of the mind.—Calvin Hall and Vernon Nordby, *The Individual and His Dreams*

EVERYONE'S DREAMS ARE DIFFERENT. WHEN WE LOOK AT A GROUP OF dreams by the same dreamer, a distinctive style emerges, much like the recognizable style of an established novelist, painter, or composer. Some people have long, intricate, convoluted dreams, while others have short and uncomplicated ones. Some dreams are strong visually, with an emphasis on colors, textures, and shapes. Others may be a string of vignettes linked by a mood. Dreams can be mostly verbal, with lots of dialogue, while others may rely on innuendo. They may be full of action, movement, and adventure. The varieties are endless. By looking at a collection of your written dreams, you can distinguish and appreciate those qualities that mark your unique dreaming style.

The major advantage of recording your dreams over a period of time is that doing so gives you the opportunity to discover significant connections between dreams that then form a series. Researchers have found that dreams over a single night tend to be related, developing variations on a single theme. Night after night the drama continues, adding new situations, images, and events, creating a constantly unfolding life story.

The view over time gives you the opportunity to gain a developing sense of yourself and the world as you perceive it. You are able to chart the growth and direction of your inner life as it parallels the changes of your waking life.

The easiest way to find a dream series is to pick out the most obvious recurring image and trace the way it develops and

Untitled, undated, Augustus Vincent Tack.

No. 114, 1960, Morris
Louis.

FACING PAGE: *Cool Note*,
1965, Adolph Gottlieb.

changes. Your personal symbol glossary, with the dated entries you
have made, will chart your course. The direction or nature of
changes in the image may alert you to the changes going on in your
waking life. Looking at a series of dreams that seem unrelated on
the surface may expose underlying patterns in your life.

Over a period of two years, one dreamer had the following series
of dreams involving a recurring image of her old beat-up Volks-
wagen Beetle. In one dream: "My VW has been damaged inexplica-
bly, having been hit from behind when no one was watching." In
another: "I go out to find the car has been towed away." In yet
another: "I am sitting in the passenger seat when the paved road
ends and the path becomes rocky and treacherous. There is no
driver."

During this time the dreamer had been having a very difficult
time at work. She felt she had been made a scapegoat in her
department and was under attack. The car symbolized herself, and
the dreams revealed her feelings of being violated ("hit from

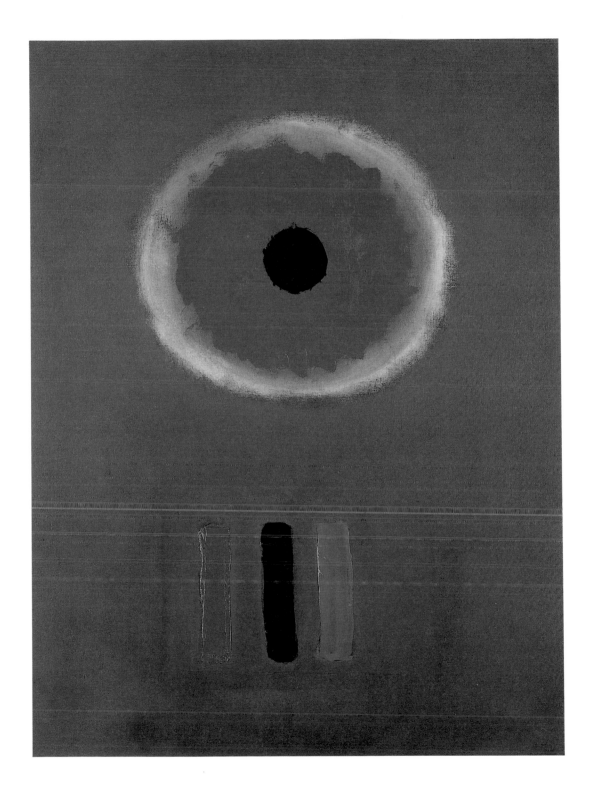

behind") and victimized ("towed away") and pointed out her passivity in handling the attacks ("There is no driver").

After she had taken steps to change the situation at work, she had the following dream: "I look down from the window of my apartment and see my VW parked in the sun. Suddenly, the car becomes a greenhouse filled with rapidly growing green plants." She had made a decision for her personal nurturance, and the dream was celebrating her action.

Once you have collected a group of about twenty dreams, you can trace the recurring images to establish patterns and series. Once you have established a pattern, a meaning will become clear. For example, if in five dreams you find yourself in an unprotected place, this is a pattern. Then look at the dream series and ask yourself under what dream conditions you leave yourself (or feel yourself) unprotected. What do these dream conditions remind you of in real life? This discovery can let you understand how you feel and behave in your waking life and can help you decide what adjustments need to be made in the future.

Think of yourself, the dreamer, as the main character in an unfolding drama. See the dreams as events and experiences in your life and then locate their parallels in waking life. Use these questions to trigger insights into your dream-life drama:

~ What kinds of roles do I play? Am I actively involved or just an observer?
~ Am I victim or aggressor? Am I leader or follower?
~ Do my roles change over time?
~ In what kinds of settings do I usually place myself? Are they indoors or outdoors? hospitable or hostile? familiar or strange? past or present?
~ In what kinds of situations do I most often find myself— pleasurable, challenging, threatening, exciting, frustrating?
~ Am I usually alone or with others? Are other people helpful? demanding? loving? rejecting?

- → What people appear repeatedly in my dreams? What aspects of myself might they represent?
- → What objects appear repeatedly? Does the image of that object change from dream to dream over time? In what ways? Do I sense a direction in those changes?
- → Might I have a recurring symbol for myself? Could it be my house? my car? my cat or dog?
- → What feelings recur in my dreams—anxiety, anger, joy, guilt, security, peacefulness? In what kinds of situations does this predominant emotion tend to occur?
- → How do I deal with conflicts or problems in my dreams? Do I confront them directly, sidestep them, run away, or call for help? To what extent are these strategies for dealing with issues successful, effective, fulfilling, self-defeating, frustrating?

Once you have identified patterns and their implications, you can begin to assess how they apply to the patterns in your waking life. Do your observations about yourself as a dream character reveal aspects of yourself that you were unaware of? This kind of insight can let you make helpful changes in the way you live. It can point at aspects of your waking life that need more attention and can suggest alternative strategies you can employ in dealing with problems.

Remember:

- → Locate recurring images to identify patterns.
- → Let meanings emerge from the patterns.
- → Ask yourself in what ways those patterns parallel your waking life.
- → Determine how these insights could be used to make changes in your waking life.

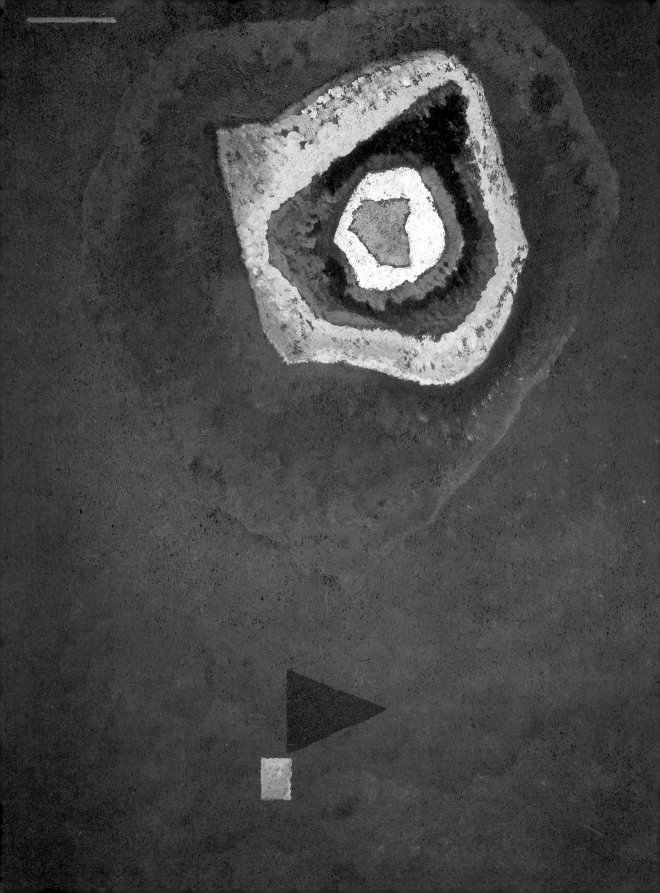

SENDING MESSAGES TO YOUR DREAMS

W*e do not sleep merely to live, but to learn to live well.*—**Synesius** of Cyrene

THE MORE YOU REMEMBER AND WORK ACTIVELY WITH YOUR DREAMS, THE more you appreciate that the dreaming and waking minds are really one. Working together, they can change your life, increasing your efficiency, enhancing your creativity, solving problems both practical and theoretical. Not only can you receive immensely valuable insights from your dreams, but you can actively enlist their aid in fulfilling your specific wants and needs.

Many societies, ancient and modern, have discovered the secrets of sending messages to the dreaming mind and reaping its benefits. These societies recognize the potential of dreams to enrich the individual and the entire society. Their attitudes and techniques have much to teach us.

A technique used by ancient cultures as varied as the Egyptians, Greeks, Hebrews, Muslims, Japanese, and Chinese is known as dream "Incubation." When you suggest to yourself before falling asleep that you will dream and remember your dreams, you are actually using the technique of incubation.

As practiced by the ancients, however, incubation was far more refined and productive. To honor their god of dreams, the ancient Egyptians erected temples that served as sacred sleeping places for those on a dream quest. Believing that dreams were messages from the gods, they expected that chosen dreamers could have their most important questions answered if the conditions were right. The process involved ritual purification, sometimes fasting and sacrifice, and ceremonies to prepare the dreamer and cleanse the sleeping space. Professional interpreters were often engaged to decode the messages supplied by the resultant dreams.

Cool Concentration (Kühle Verdichtung), 1930, Wassily Kandinsky.

The Greeks adopted the techniques of dream incubation, but dedicated their sleeping temples to Aesclapius, the god of healing. The information they sought was more specialized, related to finding specific cures and treatments for dreamers' maladies.

You need not believe that dreams are messages from the gods for the technique of incubation to work for you. You need only believe in the power and wisdom of your own unconscious. Modified to adapt to contemporary life, incubation can be a powerful tool, providing helpful and creative solutions to specific problems. Once I misplaced a student's term paper. Search as I might I was unable to locate it. That night I asked my unconscious for help and fell asleep wondering where the term paper was. I had a dream in which a stack of newspapers figured prominently. The next day I searched through a pile of newspapers waiting to be discarded, and there I found the term paper.

Incubating a dream requires little more than repeated and positive suggestion. Some dreamers devise a special sleeping environment—gauzy tents or painted canopies—or they sleep with special bedding in another room of the house. But incubation can be effective in your normal sleeping space if that environment is peaceful and undisturbed. By taking advantage of that highly suggestible state between waking and sleeping, you can induce a feeling of relaxation and meditation. Concentrate intensively on a particular problem. Formulate what you want to know into a question, and repeat that question over and over in your mind, thus programming your dreaming mind to take over when you fall asleep. Remember that success in using this technique takes time. It is a skill that takes practice and faith but the results are well worth the effort.

Dreams have been credited as the source of some famous inventions in history. Elias Howe figured out where to place the hole in the needle of his lockstitch sewing machine in a dream. Mendeleev's periodic law of the elements came to him as a dream vision. Kekulé discovered the circular molecular structure of benzene while dreaming. We do not know whether these scientists actually used the incubation technique to find solutions, but surely the intense concentration in their waking minds programmed their dreaming minds to keep working on the problem during sleep.

The most sophisticated use of communicating with one's dreams is attributed to the Senoi people of Malaysia. Studied before World

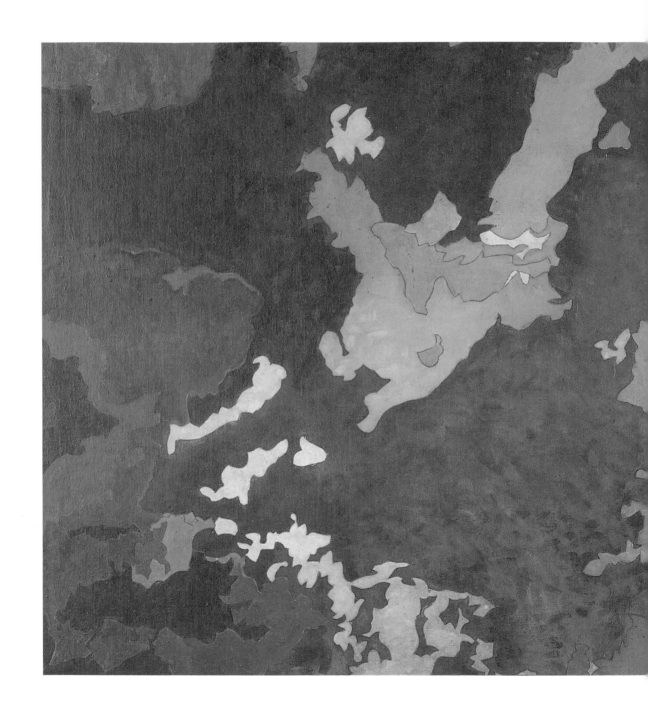

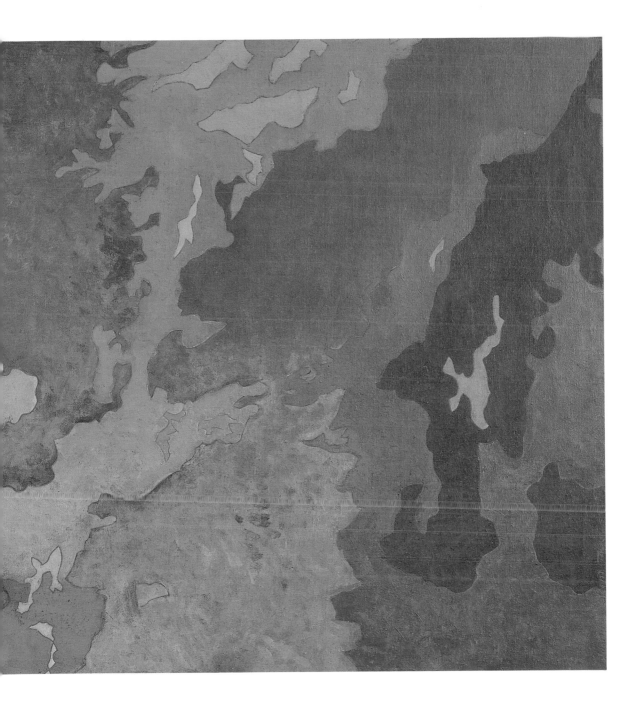

War II by anthropologist Kilton Stewart, the Senoi were described as peaceful, free of neurotic and psychotic behavior, cooperative, nonpossessive and sharing, extraordinarily self-expressive and artistically creative. Recently some experts have called Stewart's reports into question, but the fact remains that techniques inspired by his work yielded exceptional results.

Stewart believed that the Senoi's use of dreams was the key to their idyllic existence. Most of the work in this society was carried out cooperatively, in very little time, leaving much of the day free for activities in which dreams occupied a central role. Every morning over breakfast the children in each family were encouraged to tell their dreams in detail. The parents listened carefully, commending the children on the quality of their dreams and instructing them on how they should have behaved in certain dream situations. Later, the fathers and adolescent boys related their dreams at a council meeting, receiving interpretation and instruction from the society's elders.

Beginning very early on, Senoi children were instructed in the proper ways to use their dreams. If, for example, they dreamed of being chased by a monster, they were instructed that the next time they should not run away but should turn and face the monster. If attacked, they should fight, carrying on alone as long as possible but calling on "dream friends" to come to their aid when necessary. Children were thus taught to face their fears and anxieties rather than run from them; over time, a child's bad dreams would cease altogether.

Ironically, bad dreams are the ones we most often remember. They wake us up, leaving a vivid imprint. They are likely to be a part of growth, a result of taking on new challenges, risks, and change. If we adopt the Senoi technique of strongly suggesting to ourselves that we will confront the source of terror rather than run from it, we may be able to turn frightening dreams into maturing experiences.

The Senoi taught that all experiences can have positive, creative consequences. They were encouraged to bring back from their dreams new songs, dances, or designs and recreate them in waking life for the enrichment of the entire society. Trying to control your dreams defeats their potential. The Senoi techniques as adapted here do not try to control or manipulate but advocate provoking the dreaming mind with suggestions and questions that let the dream offer its own solutions. The dream's freedom and unhampered spontaneity can then provide the insight and wisdom of the unconscious and present solutions not available to us in our waking state. Following the Senoi approach, we can, by continuous self-suggestion, allow ourselves to seek options in our dreams and set models for our waking lives.

You can learn to send messages to your dreams and to tap the power of your unconscious by practicing these techniques:

↝ Make time for your dream work.
↝ Formulate specific questions for your dreams to answer and repeat them as you fall asleep.
↝ Think of your dreams as sources of gifts and re-create those gifts in your waking life.
↝ As you fall asleep, suggest to yourself that you will have pleasurable and positive experiences in your dreams.

EXTENDING YOUR JOURNAL

L*earn from your dreams what you lack.*—W. H. Auden, "The Sea and the Mirror"

ONCE YOUR JOURNAL HAS HELPED YOU ESTABLISH A DIALOGUE WITH YOUR unconscious, you may wish to start or join a dream group. Or you may feel inspired to pursue more creative activities in your life. Your dream journal will remain a valuable personal resource.

Ocean Park #110, 1978, Richard Diebenkorn.

Dream Sharing. Dreaming is an intimate experience, as each dreamer calls upon unique memories, experiences, and feelings. But dream language also draws upon archetypal and cultural references, such as myths, fairy tales, and folk tales, as well as on movies, music, and art that are shared by many people in a society. Sharing your dreams with others is an astounding experience because images that you thought private or obscure often strike common chords in others. The language of dreams is a universal, symbolic language of the imagination, expressing and interpreting human experience. Another person's intuitive response to your dream image can greatly enrich your insights into your own dream.

Try working with a dream partner, or sharing dreams with the family at breakfast, or joining a group of interested people to form a dream community. Dream groups work best with five or six members who meet for a two- or three-hour session each week. Sometimes just reading a dream record aloud can make you think of an association that had not been apparent before. The members may learn as much about themselves by the way they respond to your dream as you learn from their comments on it. Honesty and mutual interest among group members can encourage an emotional closeness and a profound understanding rarely found in ordinary relationships.

One way of working with dreams in groups is called Dream Appreciation, a technique developed by the psychiatrist Montague Ullman. One member presents a dream and then sits back while the others respond to the dream as if it were their own. They name the feelings evoked by the dream and explore their associations to the images and metaphors. The dreamer uses these projections, relating them to the real-life events surrounding the dream. Then the dreamer and the group together explore the dream's meanings and reconstruct the sequence of the dream. The process may be taken one step further if the group wishes to explore, Senoi-like, what the dreamer could have done to reach a desirable outcome.

Overcoming Writer's Block. When you begin your day writing dreams, there is an immediate flow of imagistic thinking and poetic connections that, like priming the pump, can get you started writing. Especially if you write fiction, plays, or poetry, you can build on the dream's content and mood, develop characters and situations, and utilize details of setting in your own work. A particularly useful exercise, both for creativity and personal insight, is to rewrite dreams, either by reworking their endings or by writing from another character's point of view.

Creating Art. Dreams have been the source of inspiration for countless artists. Giuseppe Tartini composed the "Devil's Trill" sonata from a dream. Robert Louis Stevenson credited his fiction to "Brownies" who supposedly worked while he slept. Samuel Taylor Coleridge took his poem "Kubla Khan" directly from a dream. William Blake used dream visions in his sketches. By working within the context and mood of your dreams, you can guide yourself back into that dream state where the imagination has free rein.

PERSONAL SYMBOL GLOSSARY

A to Z

B

B

C

D

D

E

H

I

J

K

L

M

M

N

N

O

P

P

P

Q

R

S

S

T

T

U

V

W

X

Y

Z

PHOTO CREDITS

The type in this book was set in Fenice Light by Trufont Typographers, Hicksville, New York.

The book was printed and bound by Toppan Printing Co., Ltd., Tokyo, Japan.